MW00744077

New York is a different country.
Maybe it ought to have
a separate government. Everybody
thinks differently, they just
don't know what the hell the
rest of the United States is.

- Henry Ford -

WHITE STAR PUBLISHERS

New York is the meeting place
of the peoples, the only city
where you can hardly find
a typical American.

- Djuna Barnes -

Make your mark in New York and you are a made man.

– Mark Twain –

Once you have lived in New York
and it has become your home, no place
else is good enough. All of everything
is concentrated here, population, theater,
art, writing, publishing, importing, business,
murder, mugging, luxury, poverty.
It is all of everything. It goes all right.
It is tireless.

- John Steinbeck -

New York City, the incomparable,
the brilliant star city of cities,
the forty-ninth state, a law unto itself,
the Cyclopean Paradox, the inferno
with no-out-of bounds, the supreme
expression of both the miseries
and the splendors of contemporary
civilization, the Macedonia of the United
States. It meets the most severe test
that may be applied to the definition of
a metropolis - it stays up all night.
But also it becomes a small town
when it rains.

- John Gunther -

You don't have to be born in New York City to be a New Yorker. You have to live here for six months. And if at the end of the six months you walk faster, you talk faster, you think faster, you're a New Yorker.

— Edward I. Koch —

Over the great bridge, with the sunlight
through the girders making a constant flicker
upon the moving cars, with the city rising
up across the river in white heaps and sugar
lumps all built with a wish out
of non-olfactory money.

- F. Scott Fitzgerald -

One belongs to New York instantly,
one belongs to it as much
in five minutes as in five years.

- Thomas Wolfe -

I get out of the taxi
and it's probably the
only city which in reality
looks better than on the
postcards, New York.

- Milos Forman -

At night ... the streets become
rhythmical perspectives of
glowing dotted lines, reflections
hung upon them in the streets
as the wistaria hangs
its violet racemes on its trellis.
The buildings are shimmering
verticality, a gossamer veil,
a festive scene-prop hanging
there against the black sky
to dazzle, entertain, amaze.

– Frank Lloyd Wright –

New York is the biggest collection
of villages in the world.

- Alistair Cooke -

New York is to the nation what the
white church spire is to the village -
the visible symbol of aspiration and faith,
the white plume saying the way is up!

- E.B. White -

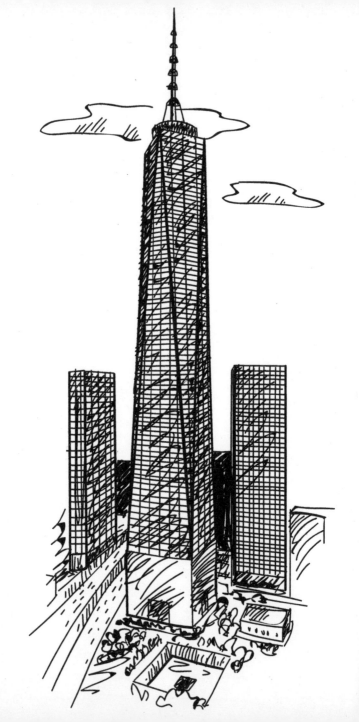

I remember how often some
of us walked out of the darkness
of the Lower East Side
and into the brilliant sunlight
of Washington Square.

- Harry Golden -

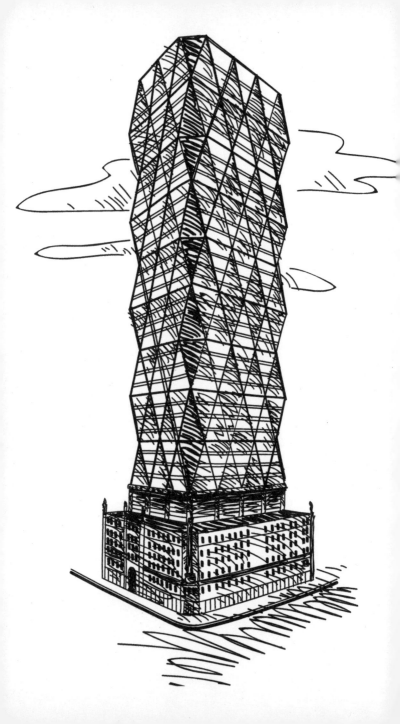

A hundred times have I thought New York is a catastrophe, and fifty times: It is a beautiful catastrophe.

- Le Corbusier -

Sometimes, from beyond
the skyscrapers, the cry of a tugboat
finds you in your insomnia,
and you remember that this desert
of iron and cement is an island.

– Albert Camus –

New York is made up of
millions of different people,
and they all come here
looking for something.

– Lindsey Kelk –

Whenever spring comes
to New York I can't stand
the suggestion of the land that
come blowing over the river from
New Jersey and I've got to go.
So I went.

- Jack Kerouac -

And New York is the most
beautiful city in the world?
It is not far from it.
No urban night is like the night
there . . . Squares after squares
of flame, set up and cut into
the aether. Here is our poetry,
for we have pulled down
the stars to our will.

– Ezra Pound –

Give me such shows — give me
the streets of Manhattan!

— Walt Whitman —

New York is the only real city-city.

- Truman Capote -

It is the vision of a great metropolis,
pulsing with endless life, which beats to
the rhythm of an immense heart, a rhythm
understandable in the four corners
of the world. One of the most impressive
and evocative visions which one can live.

– Theodore Dreiser –

THE·TRUE·ADMINISTRATION·OF·JUSTICE·IS·THE·FIRMEST·PILLAR·OF·GOOD·GOVERNMENT

New York flaunts a power that is real as its financial power, as its great enterprise ability, as its dynamism.

- Corrado Augias -

I believe in New Yorkers.
Whether they've ever questioned
the dream in which they live,
I wouldn't know, because
I won't ever dare ask
that question.

- Dylan Thomas -

As for New York City, it is a place apart.
There is not its match
in any other country in the world.

- Pearl S. Buck -

There is something in the New York
air that makes sleep useless.

- Simone de Beauvoir -

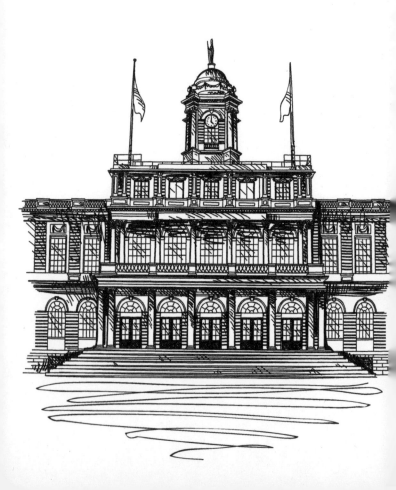

It isn't like the rest of the country
- it is like a nation itself - more
tolerant than the rest in a curious way.
Littleness gets swallowed up here.
All the viciousness that makes
other cities vicious is sucked up
and absorbed in New York.

- John Steinbeck -

I have looked down across the city
from high windows. It is then that
the great buildings lose reality and
take on their magical powers.
They are immaterial; that is to say,
one sees but the lighted windows.

- Ezra Pound -

I go to Paris, I go to London,
I go to Rome, and I always say,
There's no place like New York.
It's the most exciting city in the
world now. That's the way it is.
That's it.

– Robert De Niro –

East Side, West Side,
all around the town,
The tots sang Ring-a-rosie,
"London Bridge is falling Down;"
Boys and Girls together,
me and Mamie O'Rourke,
Tripped the light fantastic
on the sidewalks of New York.

- James W. Blake -

I can't with any conscience argue
for New York with anyone.
It's like Calcutta. But I love
the city in an emotional, irrational
way, like loving your mother
or your father even though they're
a drunk or a thief. I've loved
the city my whole life — to me,
it's like a great woman.

- Woody Allen -

Allen, Woody, *1935-, American director, screenwriter, actor, writer and playwright*

Augias, Corrado, *1935-, Italian journalist, writer, host and politician*

Barnes, Djuna, *1892-1982, American writer*

Blake, James W., *1862-1935, English singer-songwriter*

Buck, Pearl S., *1892-1973, American writer, screenwriter and academician*

Camus, Albert, *1913-1960, French writer, philosopher, essayist and dramatist*

Capote, Truman, *1924-1984, American writer, screenwriter, playwright and actor*

Cooke, Alistair, *1908-2004, American journalist*

de Beauvoir, Simone, *1908-1986, French writer, essayist and philosopher*

De Niro, Robert, *1943-, American actor, director and filmmaker*

Dreiser, Theodore, *1871-1945, American writer and journalist*

Fitzgerald, F. Scott, *1896- 1940, American writer and screenwriter*

Ford, Henry *1863-1947, American businessman*

Forman, Milos, *1932-, Czech director, screenwriter and actor*

Golden, Harry, *1902-1981, Jewish-American writer and journalist*

Gunther, John, *1901-1970, American journalist*

Kelk, Lindsey, *1980-, British writer*

Kerouac, Jack, *1922-1969, American writer and poet*

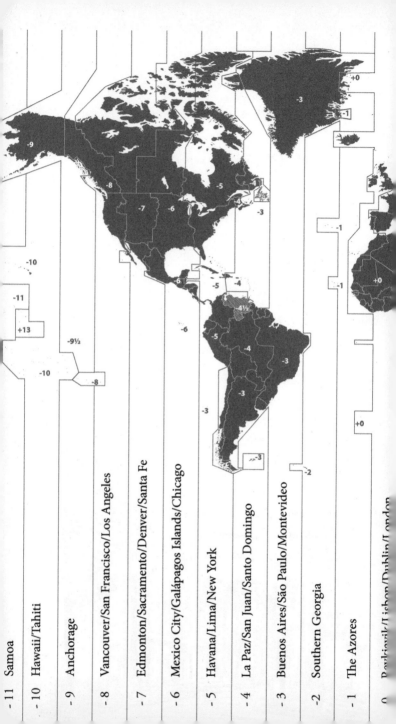

- 11 Samoa

- 10 Hawaii/Tahiti

- 9 Anchorage

- 8 Vancouver/San Francisco/Los Angeles

- 7 Edmonton/Sacramento/Denver/Santa Fe

- 6 Mexico City/Galápagos Islands/Chicago

- 5 Havana/Lima/New York

- 4 La Paz/San Juan/Santo Domingo

- 3 Buenos Aires/São Paulo/Montevideo

- 2 Southern Georgia

- 1 The Azores

  0 Reykjavik/Lisbon/Dublin/London

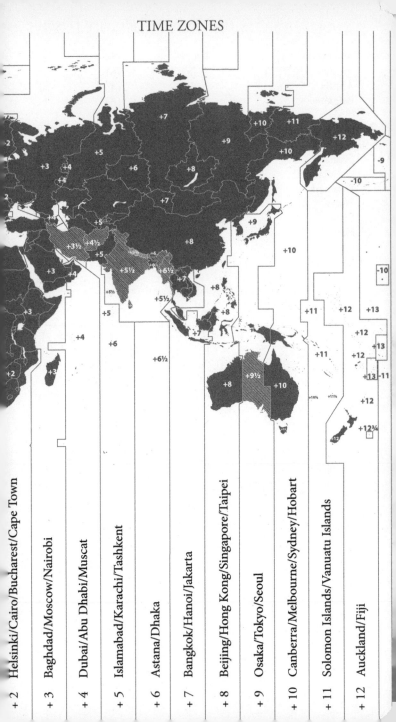

TIME ZONES

LICENSE PLATES, AREA CODES, DOMAINS,

Argentina	RA	+54	.ar
Australia	AUS	+61	.au
Austria	A	+43	.at
Belgium	B	+32	.be
Brazil	BR	+55	.br
Canada	CDN	+1	.ca
China	CN	+86	.cn
Croatia	HR	+385	.hr
Denmark	DK	+45	.dk
Finland	FIN	+358	.fi
France	F	+33	.fr
Germany	D	+49	.de
Greece	GR	+30	.gr
Hong Kong	HK	+852	.hk
Hungary	H	+36	.hu
India	IND	+91	.in
Ireland	IRL	+353	.ie
Iceland	IS	+354	.is
Israel	IL	+972	.il
Italy	I	+39	.it
Japan	J	+81	.jp
Malaysia	MAL	+60	.my
Mexico	MEX	+52	.mx
Netherlands	NL	+31	.nl
New Zealand	NZ	+64	.nz
Norway	N	+47	.no
Poland	PL	+48	.pl
Portugal	P	+351	.pt
Romania	RO	+40	.ro
Russia	RUS	+7	.ru
Slovakia	SK	+421	.sk
Slovenia	SLO	+386	.si
South Africa	ZA	+27	.za
South Korea	ROK	+82	.kr
Spain	E	+34	.es
Sweden	S	+46	.se
Switzerland	CH	+41	.ch
Turkey	TR	+90	.tr
United Kingdom	GB	+44	.uk
United States of America	USA	+1	.us

LANGUAGES AND CURRENCY

Spanish	Argentine peso
English	Australian dollar
German	Euro
French (Walloon), Dutch (Flemish) and German	Euro
Portuguese	Brazilian real
English and French	Canadian dollar
Chinese	Chinese renminbi
Croatian	Croatian kuna
Danish	Danish krone
Finnish and Swedish	Euro
French	Euro
German	Euro
Greek	Euro
Chinese and English	Hong Kong dollar
Hungarian	Hungarian Forint
Hindi and English	Indian rupee
Irish Gaelic and English	Euro
Icelandic	Icelandic króna
Hebrew and Arabic	New shekel
Italian	Euro
Japanese	Japanese yen
Malay	Malaysian ringgit
Spanish	Mexican peso
Dutch and Frisian	Euro
English and Māori	New Zealand dollar
Norwegian	Norwegian krone
Polish	Polish złoty
Portuguese	Euro
Romanian	Romanian leu
Russian	Russian ruble
Slovak	Euro
Slovene, Italian and Hungarian	Euro
English and Afrikaans	South African rand
Korean South	Korean won
Spanish	Euro
Swedish	Swedish krona
German, French, Italian and Romansh	Swiss franc
Turkish	New Turkish lira
English	Pound sterling
English	United States dollar

Men

Shirts

USA	14½	15	15½	16	16½	17
GB	14½	15	15½	16	16½	17
D	37	38	39	40	41	42
F	37	38	39	40	41	42
I	37	38	39	40	41	42

Suits/Coats

USA	36	38	40	42	44	46
GB	36	38	40	42	44	46
D	40	42	44	46	48	50
F	42	44	46	48	50	52
I	46	48	50	52	54	56

Jeans

USA	32	33	34	35	36	38
GB	32	33	34	35	36	38
D	32	33	34	35	36	38
F	32	33	34	35	36	38
I	32	33	34	35	36	38

Shoes

USA	8½	9	9½	10	10½	11
GB	8	8½	9	9½	10	10½
D	40	41	42	43	44	45
F	40	41	42	43	44	45
I	40	41	42	43	44	45

Length
1 in = 2.54 cm
0.3937 in = 1 cm
1 SM = 1.6093 km
0.6214 SM = 1 km
1 NM = 1.8519 km
0.5400 NM = 1 km

Area
1 ac = 0.4047 ha
2.471 ac = 1 ha
1 SM² = 2.5900 km²
0.3861 SM² = 1 km²

Women

Shirts

USA	4	6	8	10	12	14
GB	6	8	10	12	14	16
D	32	34	36	38	40	42
F	34	36	38	40	42	44
I	38	40	42	44	46	48

Dresses/Suits

USA	4	6	8	10	12	14
GB	6	8	10	12	14	16
D	32	34	36	38	40	42
F	34	36	38	40	42	44
I	38	40	42	44	46	48

Jeans

USA	4	6	6-8	8-10	10	12
GB	25	27	28	29	30	32
D	25	27	28	29	30	32
F	25	27	28	29	30	32
I	25	27	28	29	30	32

Shoes

USA	6	6½	7½	8½	9	9½
GB	3½	4	5	6	6½	7
D	36	37	38	39	40	41
F	35	36	37	38	39	40
I	36	37	38	39	40	41

Weight
oz = 28.349 g
g = 0.03527 oz
lb = 0.4536 kg
kg = 2.205 lb

Volume
1 (USA) gal = 3.7854 l
0.2642 (USA) gal = 1 l
1 (GB) gal = 4.5460 l
0.2200 (GB) gal = 1 l

Temperature
0 °C = 32 °F

Speed
1 mph = 1.6 km/h

Illustrated by
Marisa Vestita

Graphic design
Valentina Giammarinaro

WHITE STAR PUBLISHERS

WS White Star Publishers® is a registered trademark
property of White Star s.r.l.

© 2017 White Star s.r.l.
Piazzale Luigi Cadorna, 6
20123 Milan, Italy
www.whitestar.it

Translation: Iceigeo, Milan

ISBN 978-88-544-1119-7
1 2 3 4 5 6   21 20 19 18 17

Printed in Italy by Rotolito Lombarda - Seggiano di Pioltello (MI)